THE JAPANESE FOOD BIBLE

100 YUMMY AND FLAVORY RECIPES

GRAYSON JOSHUA

Disclaimer

The information contained i is meant to serve as a comprehensive collection of strategies that the author of this eBook has done research about. Summaries, strategies, tips and tricks are only recommendation by the author, and reading this eBook will not guarantee that one's results will exactly mirror the author's results. The author of the eBook has made all reasonable effort to provide current and accurate information for the readers of the eBook. The author and it's associates will not be held liable for any unintentional error or omissions that may be found. The material in the eBook may include information by third parties. Third party materials comprise of opinions expressed by their owners. As such, the author of the eBook does not assume responsibility or liability for any third party material or opinions. Whether because of the progression of the internet, or the unforeseen changes in company policy and editorial submission guidelines, what is stated as fact at the time of this writing may become outdated or inapplicable later.

INTRODUCTION

The Japanese have always enjoyed the attention of the world, all thanks to their enviable technology array. And their cuisine is another area of great admiration by many but not everyone has a grasp of pantry creativity. Well, that is about to change because you will be toured around 50 incredible and easy Japanese dishes to make at home. With this, you can finally close your eyes and enjoy endless Japanese aroma in the air.

Japanese cooking mainly includes the territorial and conventional nourishments of Japan, which have been developed through hundreds of years of political, monetary, and social changes. The customary cooking of Japan depends on rice with miso soup and different dishes; there is an accentuation on seasonal ingredients.

There are various different kinds of spices being used in Japanese cooking, out of which many have been discussed in detail in the chapters below. You will learn different recipes, including breakfast, lunch, dinner, dessert, salad, soups, snacks, sushi, alternative, and traditional as well as vegetarian recipes.

All the recipes mentioned in this book are extremely easy to make all on your own at home. Now, let us not brag too much and finally start cooking Japanese at home.

BREAKFAST

1. Nori deviled egg

Ingredients

- 7 large hardboiled eggs. Cracked and cut in halves
- 4 nori sheets. Cut into strips
- ½ cup mayonnaise
- 2tsp. rice vinegar
- 2tsp. wasabi paste
- ¼ tsp. sea salt

Ingredients

a) Remove yolk from eggs and mash
b) Add the mashed yolk to mayo, salt, wasabi, vinegar, and mix to a perfect paste
c) Arrange the egg whites on a plate
d) Scoop and drop content inside the well of each egg white
e) Wet the nori strips and place them on each stuffed egg

2. Tamagoyaki; bento box rolled omelet

Ingredients

- 2 large eggs
- ½ nori
- 1 ½ tsp. white sugar
- 1tsp. milk
- 2tsp. chopped carrots
- 2tsp. finely chopped spring onions
- 2tbsp. canola oil

Instructions

a) In a clean small bowl, whisk the egg, milk, sugar, and nori. Set aside

b) Heat the oil in a large clean nonstick skillet

c) Toss in and fry the onions and carrots for 1 minute

d) Remove from the heat and pour content into the egg mixture. Stir well and pour back into the greased saucepan

e) When the egg begins to form, roll it over to form a wrap

f) Sauté for 2 minutes, allowing it to cook through

g) Transfer to a flat plate and cut into rolls

h) Have fun!

3. Dorayaki, fluffy Japanese pancakes

Ingredients

- 1 cup. Self-rising flour
- A pinch of salt
- $\frac{1}{4}$ tsp. cinnamon powder
- 3 large eggs.
- $\frac{1}{2}$ tsp. baking soda
- $\frac{1}{2}$ cup sugar or honey
- 4tbsp. milk
- $\frac{1}{2}$ pound Anko (sweet azuki bean puree)
- 2cup. Vegetable oil for frying

Instructions

a) Add sugar to the cracked eggs and beat it till blended

b) Have the baking soda dissolved in water and add it to the egg mixture

c) Fold in the sieved flour gradually while stirring for a better incorporation

d) Brush a nonstick skillet with some oil and heat it

e) Pour a scoopful of batter into the skillet and fry. Flip over to make the other side

f) Remove when lightly tanned

g) Fry the remaining batter similarly

h) When ready, scoop and place Anko bean paste on each pancake and cover with another. Make a sandwich.

4. Japanese Omelette

Serving Size: 1

Ingredients:

- Soy sauce, one tbsp.
- Eggs, four
- Sugar, one tbsp.
- Mirin, one tbsp.
- Salt, as required
- Cooking oil, as required

Method:

a)   Add one tablespoon each of soy sauce, mirin and sugar and a little salt to your egg mix.

b)   Put a small amount of cooking oil in your pan and bring it up to medium heat. Keep some kitchen roll handy to help keep the pan oiled during cooking.

c)   Add a small amount of your egg mix into the heated pan. Once the egg is cooked slightly so that the top is still slightly uncooked, push it over to the side of your pan.

d)   Add a little more oil to the pan using the kitchen roll and add another small amount of the egg mix to your pan.

e)   You can then begin to roll the first bit of egg over the mix you just put in the pan until you have a small roll of egg.

5. Japanese Style Pancakes

Serving Size: 4

Ingredients:

- Milk, one and a half cup
- Baking powder, two tsp.
- Sugar, three tbsp.
- Kosher salt, half tsp.
- Unsalted butter, four tbsp.
- Eggs, four
- Vanilla extract, one tsp.
- Cream of tartar, a quarter tsp.
- Maple syrup, as required
- All-purpose flour, one and a half cup

Method:

a) Whisk together the flour, sugar, baking powder and salt in a large bowl.

b) Whisk together the milk, melted butter, vanilla and egg yolk in a medium bowl until combined.

c) Beat the egg whites and cream of tartar in another large bowl.

d) Stir the milk mixture into the flour mixture until just combined. Then gently fold in the remaining egg whites until just combined.

e) Put the prepared ring moulds in the middle of the skillet and fill each with half cup of batter.

f) Cook until golden on both sides.

6. Japanese Breakfast Rice Bowl

Serving Size: 1

Ingredients:

- Egg, one
- Thinly sliced nori, as required
- Hondashi, a pinch
- Mirin, half tsp.
- Soy sauce, half tsp.
- MSG, a pinch
- Furikake, as required
- Cooked white rice, one cup

Method:

a) Place rice in a bowl and make a shallow scoop in the centre.

b) Break the whole egg into the centre.

c) Season with half teaspoon soy sauce, a pinch of salt, a pinch of MSG, half teaspoon mirin, and a pinch of Hondashi.

d) Stir vigorously with chopsticks to incorporate egg; it should become pale yellow, frothy, and fluffy in texture.

e) Taste and adjust seasonings as necessary.

f) Sprinkle with furikake and nori, make a small scoop in the top, and add the other egg yolk.

g) Your dish is ready to be served.

7. Tamagoyaki

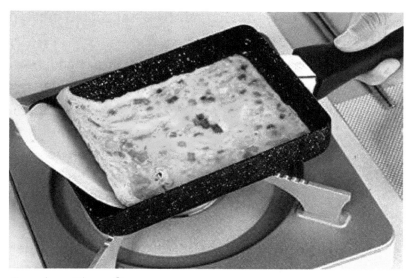

Serving Size: 2

Ingredients:

- Eggs, three

- Olive oil, one tsp.
- Shirodashi, two tsp.
- Salt, pinch
- Water, two tbsp.

Method:

a) Crack the eggs into a medium size mixing bowl.

b) Add seasoning and mix them all together gently to avoid too much bubble forming.

c) Strain the egg mixture through a sieve a few times.

d) Pour about two tbsp. oil in a small bowl and soak kitchen paper and set aside.

e) Heat two tsp. olive oil in the frying pan over medium heat till you can feel the heat when you hover your hand over the pan.

f) Pour a quarter of egg mixture into the pan.

g) Break any bubbles that have been formed with the edge of the chopsticks and scramble gently and slightly.

8. Tonkatsu

Serving Size: 4

Ingredients:

- Eggs, two
- Flour, as required
- Tonkatsu sauce, for serving
- Shredded Napa cabbage, as required
- Bread crumbs, as required
- Pork loins, four pieces
- Oil, for frying
- Salt, pinch
- Pepper, as required

Method:

a) Pound to flatten the loin cutlet to about a quarter inch. Salt and pepper both sides of each cutlet.

b) Dredge each in flour, then dip into beaten eggs and press into bread crumbs to coat both sides.

c) Heat a large skillet with about half inch of oil until hot.

d) Lay the cutlets in the hot oil. Deep-fry until golden brown.

e) Drain the cutlets on paper towels and cut the pork into bite-size strips that can be eaten with chopsticks.

f) Arrange the pork on a platter lined with the shredded cabbage, and garnish with lemon wedges.

9. Japanese Egg Omelette Sandwich

Serving Size: 2

Ingredients:

- Eggs, two
- Japanese soup stock, half tsp.
- Hot water, one tsp.
- Soy sauce, one tsp.
- Mayonnaise, as required
- Bread slices, four
- Oil, for frying
- Salt, pinch
- Pepper, as required

Method:

a) Melt the Japanese soup stock in hot water, and keep it cool.

b) Mix all ingredients using a whisk.

c) Put oil thinly to a 12 cm × 12 cm heat-resistant container.

d) Wrap the container and warm one minute thirty seconds with microwave.

e) Take it out and keep it cool. Wipe off extra moisture with kitchen paper.

f) Spread the mayonnaise over one side of breads. Put on omelette and cut it into four pieces.

g) Your dish is ready to be served.

10. Japanese Rolled Omelette

Serving Size: 4

Ingredients:

- Eggs, six
- Daikon, for serving
- Soy sauce, one tsp.
- Salt, one tsp.
- Mirin, one tbsp.
- Caster sugar, one tbsp.
- Shiso leaves, as required
- Oil, for frying

Method:

a) Mix the dashi stock with mirin, sugar, soy sauce, and salt.

b) Add to the beaten eggs and stir well. Heat the omelette pan over medium heat.

c) Pour in some egg mixture and tilt the pan to coat evenly.

d) Keep the rolled omelette in the pan and push it back to the farthest side from you.

e) Again, pour in some egg mixture into the empty side, lift up the first roll with chopsticks and let the egg mixture runs underneath.

f) Repeat the process until all egg mixture is used up.

11. Hiroshima Okonomiyaki

Serving Size: 2

Ingredients:

- Water, two tbsps.
- Eggs, three
- Bacon, six strips
- Cabbage, 150g
- Okonomiyaki flour, half cup
- Okonomiyaki sauce, two tbsp.
- Bonito flakes, as required
- Yakisoba noodles, two cups
- Pickled ginger, one tsp.
- Aonori seaweed, as required

Method:

a) Mix the okonomiyaki flour with the water, and one egg until you have a smooth batter with no lumps.

b) Add just under half the batter to a pan in a nice even circle.

c) Add half of the cabbage and half of the bean sprouts on top of the batter and then bacon.

d) Pour one tbsp. of the batter on the top of the mix and let cook for about ten minutes before flipping.

e) cook one serving of yakisoba & move the okonomiyaki on top of the noodles.

f) Crack an egg in a bowl and break the yolk before pouring in the first pan to the side of the okonomiyaki.

g) Place the okonomiyaki over the egg and leave to cook for two minutes.

h) Garnish and serve.

12. Japanese Hibachi Style Fried Rice

Serving Size: 4

Ingredients:

- Toasted sesame oil, one tbsp.
- Salt, as required
- Ground black pepper, as required
- Eggs, two
- Cooked rice, four cups
- Soy sauce, two tbsp.
- Chopped onion, one
- Butter, four tbsp.

Method:

a) lightly whisk together the eggs, salt, and ground black pepper.

b) Add one tablespoon of butter into the heated wok or skillet. Once the butter melts, add in the eggs and scramble.

c) Add in another one tablespoon of butter into the heated wok. add chopped onion. Add in the remaining butter & add in the cooked rice.

d) Add in the soy sauce and toasted sesame oil with the rice.

e) Once the fried rice has been lightly browned, add in the egg and stir to evenly distribute.

f) Serve warm with some yum sauce.

13. Japanese Breakfast Skillet

Serving Size: 2

Ingredients:

- Japanese sweet potato, half cup
- Sliced carrots, half cup
- Fresh ginger, half tsp.
- Mirin, a quarter cup
- Sliced mushrooms, one cup
- Tamari, two tbsp.
- White onions, half cup
- Sesame oil, two tbsp.
- Organic tempeh, one block

- Vegetable broth, two cups

Method:

a) In a medium pot that will fit the block of tempeh, combine the tempeh and the vegetable broth and bring to a boil.

b) Immediately reduce to heat and simmer gently for fifteen minutes. When done, dice into small cubes and set aside.

c) In a large skillet, warm the oil and then add the diced potatoes and sliced carrots. Adjust heat to medium high and cook for fifteen minutes until the vegetables have a nice, golden color to them.

d) Add in the onions and tempeh and continue sautéing for about three minutes.

e) Add the cabbage, garlic, ginger and mushrooms, then give it a quick stir. The pan should be very dry.

f) Now deglaze with the mirin and tamari.

g) Stir for a few minutes to coat everything in the glaze.

h) Your dish is ready to be served.

MAIN DISH

14. Tonkatsu baked pork delight

Ingredients

- 1 ½ cup. Panko (Japanese bread crumbs or your regular bread crumbs)
- 1 large egg. Nicely beaten
- 1 ½ tbsp. neutral oil
- 3tsp. white flour
- 1tsp. kosher salt
- 1tbsp. black pepper
- 3 boneless pork loins

- Tonkatsu sauce
- Shredded cabbage (preferred quantity) for serving

Instructions

a) Preheat oven to 300 degrees
b) Toss the panko into a dry skillet and toast. Stirring and drizzling a little oil till it turns golden
c) Season the pork with the salt and pepper and toss the flour over it. Making sure all sides of the pork loins are covered with the flour
d) Dip the floured loins into the beaten egg and toss it over the cooled panko. Make sure that all sides are nicely covered with the crumbs
e) Place the pork in a baking tray and bake for 40 minutes or more depending on the thickness of it.
f) Dish into a platter and serve with your ready Tonkatsu sauce and shredded cabbage

15. Tofu in black pepper sauce

Ingredients

- 1 cup. Corn starch
- 1 $\frac{1}{2}$ tsp. white pepper
- 16oz firm tofu, perfectly drained
- 4tbsp. vegetable oil
- 1tsp. kosher salt
- 2 scallions, finely sliced
- 3 red chili peppers, seeded and nicely sliced

Instructions

a) Make sure tofu is well-drained and pat dry with a paper towel. You can press a heavy cutting board on it to get all the fluid out.

b) Slice the tofu into fine sturdy cubes

c) Mix the cornstarch with the white pepper and salt.

d) Toss the tofu into the flour mixture, take care to ensure the cubes are well covered.

e) Sit them in a Ziploc bag for 2 minutes

f) Pour the oil into a nonstick skillet, when hot, fry the tofu cubes to crispy cubes

g) Fry in batches and

h) Garnish with the sliced pepper and scallions

16. Sesame shiso rice

Ingredients

- 2 cups. cooked rice (short grain)
- 12 shiso leaves (add more leaves if you like). Finely sliced into strips
- 6 pieces umeboshi (Japanese pickled plum). Pitted and chopped
- 2tbsp. sesame seeds, nicely toasted

Instructions

a) In a clean deep bowl, combine the cooked rice, umeboshi, shiso leaves, and sesame seeds.
b) Serve

17. Japanese mushroom noodle soup

Ingredients

- 2oz Buna shimeji mushroom
- 1 bundle. Soba noodles or your preferred noodles. Boiled and drained according to Instructions
- 3tbsp. mizkan soup base
- 2 boiled eggs, cracked and halved
- 1 bunch baby bok choy or lettuce
- 2 cup. Water
- 2tsp. white sesame seeds
- Scallions, chopped

Instructions

a) In a medium saucepan, boil the water and add the soup base and baby bok choy, and mushroom. Cook for 2 minutes.

b) Dish the cooked noodle into plates/bowl. Place the egg halves and drizzle the soup over it

c) Garnish with scallions and sesame seeds

d) Serve with chopsticks

18. Japanese ginger sea bass

Ingredients

- 2tsp. miso white paste
- 6oz sea bass piece
- 1 $\frac{1}{4}$ tsp. mirin
- 1tsp. fresh ginger juice
- 1tsp. sugar
- 3tsp. sake

Instructions

a) In a clean medium bowl, combine all the ingredients except the sake. Mix well and set aside.

b) Place fish piece in the mixed content add the sake and toss till well covered

c) Sit it in the freezer for 4 hours

d) Preheat the grill and place fish on a grate

e) Grill it, toss from side to side till completely brown and cooked.

f) Transfer bass to a platter and serve

19. Japanese potato salad

Ingredients

- 2pound russet potato. Peeled, cooked, and mashed
- 3 cucumbers. Finely sliced
- $\frac{1}{4}$ tsp. sea salt
- 3tsp. rice wine vinegar
- 1tbsp. Japanese mustard
- 7tbsp. Japanese mayonnaise
- 2 carrots. Quartered and thinly sliced
- 3 hardboiled egg
- 1 red onion bulb. Finely sliced

Instructions

a) Place the sliced cucumber in a bowl, sprinkle some salt over them and leave it to stand for 12 minutes. Drain out the excess water and dry the cucumbers in a paper towel

b) In a small bowl, mix the mustard, mayo, and vinegar

c) In another large bowl, fold in the mashed potato, mayo mixture, eggs, cucumbers, and carrots. Stirring well to achieve an even mix

20. Japanese fancy teriyaki

Ingredients

- 2lb salmon
- 3tbsp. chopped green onions
- 2tbsp. black and white sesame seeds
- ½ cup extra virgin olive oil
- Teriyaki sauce
- 4tbsp. soy sauce
- 1 cup mirin
- 2 ½ cup. Sugar

Instructions

a) Make the teriyaki sauce by add all the ingredients under its heading into a saucepan and cook it under low heat till it thickens. Remove from heat and set it for cooling

b) Pour some oil into a nonstick skillet and place the salmon in there. cover the skillet and cook the salmon under moderate heat till evenly brown.

c) Dish into a platter and drizzle the teriyaki sauce over it

d) And garnish with white sesame seeds and chopped green onions

21. Soyi marinated mushrooms

Ingredients

- 4 packs of enoki mushrooms or your preferred mushroom
- 2tbsp. soy sauce
- 3tbsp. sunflower oil
- 3tbsp. rice vinegar
- 3tbsp. mitsuba. Nicely chopped
- 2 red chili pepper.
- 1rsp. Kosher salt
- 2tbsp. green shiso. Finely chopped

Instructions

a) Over low heat, pour the oil into a saucepan and heat it
b) Add the mushrooms to the hot oil and stir fry till it absorbs all the oil
c) Turn off the heat and stir in the soy sauce, vinegar, shiso, mitsuba, salt, and pepper.
d) Serve or refrigerate it when cooled.

22. Bento ramen eggs

Ingredients

- 6 large eggs
- 1tbsp. baking soda
- Seasoning sauce
- $\frac{1}{4}$ cup. Sake
- $\frac{1}{4}$ cup Mizkan Bonito flavored soup base or any soup base
- 5tbsp. soy sauce
- 4tbsp. mirin

Instructions

a) In a small saucepan, pour in water add the baking soda, bring to boil. Add the eggs and cook for 10 minutes when the water boils

b) In another saucepan, stir in all the sauce ingredients and cook for 5 minutes. Turn out the heat and sit it for cooling

c) When the egg is done, remove and ice-cool it. Crack and peel the shell, place in a container

d) Pour the cooled sauce over the eggs, making sure the eggs are completed immersed in the sauce. Leave it in the refrigerator overnight

e) When ready, remove from refrigerator slice each into half, and serve

23. Japanese eggy oyakadon

Ingredients

- 1 large boneless chicken thigh. Nicely cut to bite sizes
- 3 large eggs, beaten
- 2 ¼ tbsp. mirin
- ½ cup. Dashi
- 2 bowl. Cooked rice (short grain)
- 2 ¼ tbsp. soy sauce
- 1 large yellow onion, thinly sliced
- 1 spring onions, (green part) nicely sliced

- $\frac{1}{2}$ tsp. sugar
- 1 $\frac{1}{4}$ tbsp. Japanese sake

Instructions

a) Stir in mirin and sake in a saucepan and boil over low heat
b) Add the soy sauce, dashi, sugar, and onions. Cook for 3 minutes
c) Toss in the chicken and sauté for 5 minutes
d) Add the spring onions, drizzle in the beaten eggs, (don't stir)
e) When the egg begins to set, please turn off the heat
f) Dish your cooked rice in a bowl and pour egg content over it

24. Japanese curried balls (Kare pan)

Ingredients

- Dough
- 1cup. Panko
- 2tbsp. vegetable oil
- Curry filling
- 100g beef, minced
- 1 medium onion, chopped
- 2 potatoes, cooked and mashed
- 2tbsp. garlic powder
- 1 carrot. Finely diced
- 1tbsp. garam masala
- 60g curry roux

Instructions

a) Heat the oil in a clean medium saucepan, stir in the carrots, onions, garlic powder, and cook to tender

b) Add the beef and some water to cook for 20 minutes

c) Reduce the heat and fold in the curry and masala. Stir it to mix

d) Add the mashed potato and mix well to set

e) Preheat oven to 250 degrees

f) When the filling is cooled. Divide the dough into balls knead it on a floured surface, spoon some filling on the dough piece, and roll into a fine sturdy ball

g) Repeat same for the rest, paint each with the oil and toss the filled dough over the panko

h) Arrange dough in a ready baking tray and bake for 20 minutes

25. Onigiri

Serving Size: 3

Ingredients:

- Nori sheet, as required
- Umeboshi, one
- Soy sauce, half tsp.
- Mirin, half tsp.
- Tuna, one cup
- Japanese mayonnaise, two tbsp.
- Salted salmon, one piece
- Cooked rice, two cups

Method:

a) Cook the rice according to your rice cooker or if you do not have a rice cooker, follow the instructions here.

b) Transfer the cooked rice to a separate bowl to cool it down.

c) Prepare all the fillings that you are going to use and set aside.

d) Prepare seaweed sheet.

e) Place cling wrap over a rice bowl.

f) Place some of the cooked rice over the centre of the cling wrap.

g) Put about 1tsp of umeboshi on the centre of the rice then cover with the rice around.

h) Wrap the cling wrap over the rice and squeeze and mould the rice into a triangle shape with your hands.

i) Remove the cling wrap and cover the bottom of the rice triangle with a nori sheet.

j) Your dish is ready to be served.

26. Natto

Serving Size: 1

Ingredients:

- Scallions, for garnish
- Natto, one tbsp.
- Soy sauce, half tsp.
- Saikkyo, one and a half tsp.
- Tofu, half block
- Miso, two tbsp.
- Wakame seeds, a handful
- Dashi, two cups

Method:

a) Bring the dashi to a simmer in a soup pot and place the spoonful of natto into the liquid. Simmer for two minutes.

b) Place the miso pastes into the pot and use the back of a spoon to dissolve the pastes into the dashi.

c) Add the wakame and the tofu and simmer for 30 seconds longer.

d) Garnish with scallions.

e) Serve immediately.

27. Agedashi Tofu

Serving Size: 3

Ingredients:

- Flavoured oil, three cups
- Corn starch, four tbsp.
- Soy sauce, two tbsp.
- Katsuobishi, as required
- Tofu, one block
- Mirin, two tbsp.
- Daikon radish, as required
- Scallions, as required
- Shichimi Togarashi, a handful
- Dashi, one cup

Method:

a) Gather all the ingredients.

b) Wrap the tofu with three layers of paper towels and place another plate on top. Drain the water out of tofu for fifteen minutes.

c) Peel and grate the daikon and gently squeeze water out. Cut the green onion into thin slices.

d) Put dashi, soy sauce, and mirin in a small saucepan and bring to boil.

e) Remove the tofu from paper towels and cut it into eight pieces.

f) Coat the tofu with potato starch, leaving excess flour, and immediately deep fry until they turn light brown and crispy.

g) Remove the tofu and drain excess oil on a plate lined with paper towels or wire rack.

h) To serve, place the tofu in a serving bowl and gently pour the sauce without wetting the tofu.

28. Nasu Dengaku

Serving Size: 4

Ingredients:

- Japanese eggplant, three
- Flavoured oil, one tbsp.
- Sake, two tbsp.
- Sugar, two tbsp.
- Miso, four tbsp.
- Sesame seeds, as required
- Tofu, one block
- Mirin, two tbsp.
- Daikon radish, three
- Konnyaku, a handful

Method:

a) Combine sake, mirin, sugar, and miso in a saucepan.

b) Mix well to combine and then bring to a gentle simmer over the lowest heat. Stir constantly and cook for few minutes.

c) Wrap the tofu with two sheets of paper towel and press the tofu between two plates for 30 minutes.

d) Place the tofu and eggplants on a rimmed baking sheet lined with parchment paper or silicone baking sheet. With a brush, apply vegetable oil on top and bottom of tofu and eggplants.

e) Bake at 400 degrees for twenty minutes, or until the eggplant is tender.

f) Carefully spoon some of the miso glaze onto your tofu and eggplants and spread evenly. Broil for five minutes.

29. Omurice

Serving Size: 2

Ingredients:

- Boneless chicken, one pound
- Olive oil, one tbsp.
- Mixed vegetables, half cup
- Salt and pepper, as required
- Cooked Japanese rice, one and a half cup
- Soy sauce, one tsp.
- Ketchup, one tbsp.
- Milk, two tbsp.
- Eggs, two
- Cheese, a handful

Method:

a) Heat the oil and sauté the onion until softened. Add the chicken

b) Add the mixed vegetables and season with salt and pepper.

c) Add the rice and break into small pieces.

d) Add ketchup and soy sauce and combine everything evenly with a spatula.

e) Heat the olive oil in the pan over medium high heat.

f) When the pan is hot, pour the egg mixture into the pan and tilt to cover the bottom of the pan. Lower the heat when the bottom of the egg is set.

g) Put the cheese and the divided fried rice on top of the Omelette.

30. Okonomiyaki

Serving Size: 4

Ingredients:

- Dashi, one cup
- Oyster sauce, one tbsp.
- Nagaimo, as required
- Salt, as required
- Flour one and a half cup
- Sugar, half tsp.
- Baking powder, half tsp.
- Sliced pork belly, half pound
- Milk, two tbsp.

- Eggs, four
- Cabbage, one

Method:

a) Mix all the batter ingredients.

b) Add the grated nagaimo and dashi in the bowl.

c) Mix all together till combined.

d) Take out the batter from the refrigerator and add eggs, tempura scraps, and pickled red ginger in the bowl. Mix well until well-combined.

e) Add chopped cabbage to the batter. Mix well before adding the rest.

f) In a large pan, heat vegetable oil on medium heat. Spread the batter evenly.

g) Place the sliced pork belly on top of Okonomiyaki and cook covered for five minutes.

h) Gently press the okonomiyaki. Cover and cook for another five minutes.

31. Cheesy Ramen Carbonara

Cooking Time: 30 minutes

Serving Size: 4

Ingredients:

- Dashi, one cup
- Olive oil, one tbsp.
- Bacon slices, six
- Salt, as required
- Minced garlic, two
- Parsley, as required
- Parmesan cheese, half cup

- Milk, two tbsp.
- Eggs, two
- Ramen pack, three

Method:

a) Combine all the ingredients.
b) Boil noodles according to package instructions.
c) Save a quarter cup of cooking water to loosen sauce later, if needed. Drain noodles and toss with olive oil so that they do not stick.
d) Heat medium skillet over medium heat. Cook bacon pieces until brown and crisp. Add the noodles to the skillet and toss with the bacon until the noodles are coated in the bacon fat.
e) Beat eggs with fork and mix in parmesan cheese. Pour egg-cheese mixture to skillet and toss with bacon and noodles.

32. Yakisoba

Cooking Time: 30 minutes

Serving Size: 4

Ingredients:

- Fish sauce, two tbsp.
- Egg, one
- Soy sauce, half cup
- Cooked Japanese rice, three cups
- Tomatoes, two
- Cilantro, half cup
- Salt and pepper, to taste
- Vegetable oil, two tbsp.

- Japanese chili peppers, three
- Toasted walnuts, half cup
- Chicken breast, eight ounces
- Onion, one
- Scallions, half cup
- Minced garlic, one tsp.

Instructions:

a) When the wok is very hot, add two tsp of the oil.

b) When the oil is hot, add the chicken and cook on high until it is browned all over and cooked through.

c) Remove chicken and set aside, add the eggs, pinch of salt and cook a minute or two until done.

d) Add the remaining oil to the wok and add the onion, scallions and garlic. Stir in all the rice. Add the soy sauce and fish sauce stir to mix all the ingredients.

e) Keep stirring a few minutes, and then add egg and chicken back to the wok.

33. Baked chicken Katsu

Cooking Time: 25 minutes

Serving Size: 4

Ingredients:

- Boneless chicken breast pieces, one pound
- Panko, one cup
- All-purpose flour, half cup
- Water, one tbsp.
- Egg, one
- Salt and pepper, to taste
- Tonkatsu sauce, as required

Instructions:

a) Combine the panko and oil in a frying pan and toast over medium heat until golden brown. Transfer panko into a shallow dish and allow cooling down.

b) Butterfly the chicken breast and cut in half. Season salt and pepper on both sides of the chicken.

c) In a shallow dish, add flour and in another shallow dish, whisk together the egg and water.

d) Coat each chicken piece in the flour and shake off any excess flour. Dip into the egg mixture and then coat with the toasted panko, pressing firmly to adhere to the chicken.

e) Place the chicken pieces on the prepared baking sheet for about twenty minutes. Serve immediately or transfer to a wire rack so the bottom of the katsu does not get soggy from the moisture.

34. Hayashi Ground Beef Curry

Serving Size: 2

Ingredients:

- Onion, one
- Carrots, half cup
- Ground beef, half pound
- Canola oil, one tbsp.
- Ketchup, two tbsp.
- Salt and pepper, to taste
- Corn starch, one tsp.
- Beef broth, one cup
- Sake, one tbsp.

- Boiled egg, one

Instructions:

a) Boil egg and cut into small pieces or mash with a fork. Season well with salt and pepper.

b) Heat oil and add onions and carrots.

c) Sprinkle corn starch on top of ground beef and add to the vegetables. Add a quarter cup beef broth and break the ground beef while stirring.

d) Add beef broth, ketchup, sake, and Worcestershire sauce.

e) Mix well and cook for ten minutes or until all the liquid has evaporated. Season with salt and pepper.

f) Fry onions in a separate pan until crispy.

35. Ramen Noodle Skillet with Steak

Cooking Time: 15 minutes

Serving Size: 2

Ingredients:

- Onion, one
- Carrots, half cup
- Ground beef, half pound
- Canola oil, one tbsp.
- Ketchup, two tbsp.
- Salt and pepper, to taste
- Corn starch, one tsp.
- Beef broth, one cup

- Sake, one tbsp.
- Boiled egg, one
- Worcestershire sauce, one tbsp.

Instructions:

a) In a large skillet over medium-high heat, heat oil.
b) Add steak and sear until your desired completion, about five minutes per side for medium, then transfer to a cutting board and let it rest for five minutes, and then slice it.
c) In a small bowl, whisk together soy sauce, garlic, lime juice, honey, and cayenne until combined and set aside.
d) Add onion, peppers, and broccoli to skillet and cook until tender, then add soy sauce mixture and stir until fully coated.
e) Add cooked ramen noodles and steak and toss until combined.

36. Chicken Teriyaki

Cooking Time: 15 minutes

Serving Size: 2

Ingredients:

- Sesame oil, one tsp.
- Broccoli, for serving
- Honey, one tbsp.
- Ketchup, two tbsp.
- Salt and pepper, to taste
- Corn starch, one tsp.
- Cooked white rice, one cup
- Garlic and ginger, one tbsp.

- Boiled egg, one
- Soy sauce, one tbsp.

Instructions:

a) In a medium bowl, whisk together soy sauce, rice vinegar, oil, honey, garlic, ginger, and corn starch.

b) In a large skillet over medium heat, heat oil. Add chicken to skillet and season with salt and pepper. Cook until golden and almost cooked through.

c) Cover chicken and simmer until sauce is thickened slightly and chicken is cooked through.

d) Garnish with sesame seeds and green onions.

e) Serve over rice with steamed broccoli.

37. Japanese Salmon Bowl

Cooking Time: 30 minutes

Serving Size: 4

Ingredients:

- Chili sauce, one tsp.
- Soy sauce, one tsp.
- Rice, two cups
- Sesame oil, one tbsp.
- Ginger, two tbsp.
- Salt and pepper, to taste
- Sesame seeds, one tsp.
- Vinegar, one tsp.
- Shredded nori, as required
- Salmon, half pound

- Shredded cabbage, one cup

Instructions:

a) Place the rice, three cups of water and half teaspoon of salt in a large pot and bring to the boil and cook for fifteen minutes or until water is absorbed.

b) Place the vinegar, soy sauce, chilli sauce, sesame oil, sesame seeds and ginger in a bowl and mix well.

c) Add the salmon and gently stir until completely coated.

d) Place the shredded cabbage and sesame oil in a bowl and mix until well combined.

e) Place a large spoonful of rice in each bowl, add the cabbage and squeeze over the mayonnaise.

38. Sushi Rice/Chirashi-zushi

Ingredients:

- Japanese rice, two cups
- Rice vinegar, a quarter cup
- Salt, one tsp and Sugar, two tbsp.
- Shitake mushrooms, eight
- Sashimi, half pound
- Eggs, three & Mirin, one tsp.
- Sesame seeds, as required
- Tuna, half pound

Instructions:

a) Combine the ingredients.

b) Put rice in a large bowl and wash it with cold water.

c) Place the rice in a rice cooker and add about two cups of water. Let the rice soak in the water for at least thirty minutes. Start the cooker.

d) In a small saucepan, mix rice vinegar, sugar, and salt. Put the pan on low heat and heat until the sugar dissolves.

e) Spread the hot steamed rice into a large plate or a large bowl. Sprinkle the vinegar mixture over the rice and quickly mix into the rice using a shamoji.

f) Add shiitake to a pan, soy sauce, sugar, and mirin. Simmer shiitake on low heat until the liquid is almost gone.

g) Oil a medium skillet and pour a scoop of egg &sugar mixture and make a thin Omelette

39. Broiled Shrimp and Vegetables

Cooking Time: 10 minutes

Serving Size: 4

Ingredients:

- Lime juice, three tbsp.
- Shrimp, two pounds
- Salt and pepper, to taste
- Chili, one tbsp.
- Mix vegetables, one cup
- Sashimi, half pound
- Eggs, three
- Mirin, one tsp.

- Sesame seeds, as required

Instructions:

a) Marinate the shrimp with the spices, lime juice and olive oil.
b) Meanwhile, chop and slice the veggies.
c) Add one tablespoon of olive oil in a skillet and bring to medium heat.
d) Sauté the veggies until they obtain a golden Colour and are tender. Remove and set aside in a bowl.
e) In the same skillet, sauté the shrimp until they are fully cooked. Then return the cookies veggies to the skillet, and sauté with the shrimps for two minutes.
f) Remove and serve.

40. Chicken in a Pot/Mizutaki

Cooking Time: 10 minutes

Serving Size: 4

Ingredients:

- Negi, one
- Mizuna, four
- Napa cabbage, eight
- Carrot, half cup
- Chicken thighs, one pound
- Kombu, half pound
- Sake, one tsp.
- Ginger, one tsp.
- Sesame seeds, as required

Instructions:

a) Mix all the ingredients.

b) In a large bowl, add five cups of water, and kombu to make cold brew kombu dashi. Set aside while you prepare the chicken.

c) Fill a medium pot with water and add the bone-in, skin-on chicken thigh pieces. Turn the heat on medium-low.

d) In the cold brew kombu dashi, add the chicken thigh pieces you just rinsed.

e) Also add the chicken pieces sake, and ginger.

f) Bring it to a boil over medium heat.

g) Reduce the heat to medium-low and cook covered for thirty minutes. During this time, start preparing other ingredients. After thirty minutes, remove and discard the ginger slices.

JAPANESE SALAD

41. Japanese cucumber Salad

Cooking Time: 10 minutes

Serving Size: 8

Ingredients:

- Peanuts, half cup
- Soy sauce, three tbsp.
- Sesame oil, one tsp.
- Sugar, one tbsp.
- Wine vinegar, three tbsp.

- Small cucumber, twelve ounces
- Garlic, one
- Fresh cilantro, as required

Instructions:

a) Whisk the dressing together and be sure to taste it to adjust anything you like.

b) Finely grind the peanuts in a food processor using the pulsing button.

c) If you would like to remove part of the peel first, you can run a zesting tool down the sides, or simply run the tines of a fork down the sides to create a decorative edge.

d) Put the cucumbers in a bowl and toss with enough dressing to coat thoroughly, you may not need all of it.

e) Toss with the crushed peanuts, sprinkle with chili flakes, and top with cilantro leaves.

42. Japanese Watercress Salad

Cooking Time: 10 minutes

Serving Size: 2

Ingredients:

- Peanut butter, three tbsp.
- Rice vinegar, one tbsp.
- Honey, one tsp.
- Sugar, one tbsp.
- Wine vinegar, three tbsp.
- Watercress, six cups
- Mirin, two tbsp.

Instructions:

a) In a medium size pot, bring water, salted with one tablespoon kosher salt, to boil.

b) Put the peanut butter, honey, rice vinegar, soy sauce, and mirin in a medium bowl.

c) Rinse the watercress, drain and separate the leaves from the stems.

d) Roughly chop the stems and add to the boiling water along with the leaves.

e) Cook until the stems are tender but yielding a soft crunch.

f) Drain, rinse under cold water and softly squeeze out excess water.

g) Gently pat the watercress, dry with a paper towel and add to a mixing bowl.

h) Pour the dressing over the watercress and toss until the watercress is evenly coated.

43. Kani Salad

Cooking Time: 10 minutes

Serving Size: 4

Ingredients:

- Carrot, one medium
- Cucumber, two medium
- Ripe mango, one cup
- Japanese mayonnaise, one tbsp.
- Half lemon
- Salt and pepper to taste
- Kani, 150 g

Instructions:

a) Peel the carrots and trim off the ends.

b) Do the same with the cucumber but do not include the core with seeds.

c) Shred the crab sticks by hand by gently pressing a piece from end to end to loosen the strips and then separate each strip from one another.

d) Peel the ripe mango.

e) In a large bowl, add the cucumber, carrots, Kani, mango and Japanese mayo. Squeeze the juices of half a lemon on top and toss.

f) Season with salt and pepper as needed, and give it another toss until all ingredients are well blended.

g) Serve immediately or refrigerate until ready.

h) Serve on top of a layer of iceberg or romaine lettuce.

44. Oshitashi

Cooking Time: 5 minutes

Serving Size: 1

Ingredients:

- Spinach, one pound
- Sesame seeds, one tbsp.
- Soy sauce, one tbsp.
- Mirin, one tbsp.

Instructions:

a) Toast the sesame seeds in a skillet until lightly coloured.

b) Add the spinach to a large saucepan of boiling water and cook two to three minutes until wilted.

c) Have an ice bath ready.

d) Drain the spinach in a colander.

e) Squeeze dry and place in a bowl.

f) Mix the cooked spinach with the soy sauce, mirin and sesame seeds.

g) Serve at room temperature.

45. Japanese Cabbage Salad

Cooking Time: 5 minutes

Serving Size: 1

Ingredients:

- Coleslaw mix, one cup
- Sesame seeds, one tbsp.
- Soy sauce, one tbsp.
- Mirin, one tbsp.
- Bonito flakes, as required

Instructions:

a) Mix all the ingredients for the dressing together in a bowl and pour it over the shredded coleslaw mix.

b) Toss well and top with sesame seeds and bonito flakes.

46. Ramen Noodle Salad

Cooking Time: 15 minutes

Serving Size: 1

Ingredients:

- Cabbage and onion, one cup
- Sesame seeds, one tbsp.
- Soy sauce, one tbsp.
- Sugar, one tbsp.
- Vinegar, one tbsp.
- Butter, as required
- Ramen noodles, one pack
- Almonds, as required

Instructions:

a) Combine the oil, vinegar, sugar, and soy sauce in a jar and shake until the sugar is dissolved.

b) Melt the butter in a large skillet over medium heat. While the butter is melting, crush the ramen noodles while still inside the package.

c) Remove the seasoning packet and throw away.

d) Add the noodles, almonds, and sesame seeds to the melted butter in the skillet.

e) Sauté while stirring frequently, until the noodle mixture is golden brown.

f) Shred the cabbage and combine the cabbage and onions in a large mixing bowl. Add the noodle mixture.

g) Pour the dressing over the salad and toss well to combine.

h) Serve immediately.

47. Pork Chimichurri Salad

Cooking Time: 15 minutes

Serving Size: 2

Ingredients:

- Pork chops, one pound
- Greens, six ounces
- Cherry tomatoes, two cups
- Olive oil, one tbsp.
- Vinegar, one tbsp.
- Parsley, as required
- Chipotle, half
- Oregano leaves, as required

- Salt and pepper, as required
- Chimichurri dressing, per taste

Instructions:

a) In a food processor, combine olive oil, vinegar, parsley, oregano leaves, and chipotle. Season with salt and pepper and set aside.

b) Preheat a broiler. Line a rimmed baking sheet with foil and spray with cooking oil.

c) Place pork on the baking sheet and sprinkle both sides with salt and pepper. Broil until internal temperature reaches 145 degrees, five minutes per side. Remove pork from broiler and let it rest for five minutes.

d) Meanwhile, in a large bowl, combine greens, cherry tomatoes, cheese, and chimichurri dressing to taste. Arrange salad on plates or a platter.

e) Arrange on top of salad, drizzle with additional dressing, and serve.

48. Spring Green Salad

Cooking Time: 30 minutes

Serving Size: 4

Ingredients:

- Salad potatoes, half pound
- Petits pois, half cup
- Asparagus, half cup
- Olive oil, four tbsp.
- Pumpkin seeds, one tbsp.
- Spring onions, four
- Baby courgettes, one cup
- Whole grain mustard, as required

- Salt and pepper, as required
- Honey, per taste
- Lemon juice, as required

Instructions:

a) To make the dressing, put all the ingredients in a blender and process until smooth and emulsified.

b) Cook the potatoes in lightly salted boiling water for ten minutes, or until just tender, adding the petits pois for the last two minutes.

c) Heat a large griddle pan or heavy-based frying pan until hot. Add a tablespoon of olive oil and add the asparagus in a single layer.

d) Cook for five minutes, or until lightly charred. Remove from the pan and add to the potato mixture.

e) When hot, add the courgettes, sliced side down, and cook for five minutes. Add to the potato mixture with the lettuce and spring onions.

f) Stir the dressing then pour over the salad and mix well.

49. Japanese Corn Salad

Cooking Time: 30 minutes

Serving Size: 4

Ingredients:

- Mayonnaise, one tbsp.
- Cabbage, one
- Corn, half cup
- Sugar, one tbsp.
- Salt and pepper, as per taste
- Ground sesame seeds, two tbsp.

Instructions:

a) Shred the cabbage and drain the excess water. To allow a nice texture, do not shred it too thinly.

b) To prepare the dressing, mix the ingredients together.

c) In another bowl, mix the cabbage and corn. Add the dressing and you are done.

d) Add the dressing right before serving as the cabbage tends to get watery.

e) Your dish is ready to be served.

50. Soy cucumber sonomono

Ingredients

- 1 cucumber. Sliced
- 1 ½ tsp. kosher salt
- 2 tsp. mirin
- 4g dried seaweed mix
- 2 ¼ tsp. rice vinegar
- 2tsp. soy sauce
- 2tsp. sesame seeds (for garnishing)

Instructions

a) In a small bowl, combine the vinegar, mirin, and soy sauce; set aside

b) Place sliced cucumbers in a bowl and drizzle the salt over them. Leave it cover for 7 minutes to emit all fluid

c) Drain out the water and leave them in a bowl

d) Put the seaweed in a bowl of water, leave it to stand for 8 minutes. Drain out the water

e) Place the drained cucumber slices and seaweed in a bowl. Pour the soy mixture it, drizzle the sesame seeds

CONCLUSION

What a ride! Knowing awesome Japanese meals at once was worth the ride... and if you are planning on hosting an Asian-theme party, it is a good time to start practicing your Asian culinary skills and be proud of yourself. So, feel free to try your hands on them one by one and remember to tell us how it went.

Japanese Cuisine is known for its variety of dishes and its vast combination of rare spices that are usually grown only in Japan.

Happy Cooking Japanese Food!

JAPANESE SOUP RECIPES

51. Miso soup

Cooking Time: 15 minutes

Serving Size: 4

Ingredients:

- Water, four cups
- Miso paste, three tbsp.
- Green onions, two
- Dashi granules, two tbsp.
- Tofu, one block

Instructions:

a) In a medium saucepan over medium-high heat, combine dashi granules and water; bring to a boil.

b) Reduce heat to medium, and whisk in the miso paste, and then stir in tofu.

c) Separate the layers of the green onions, and add them to the soup.

d) Simmer gently for a few minutes before serving.

e) Your soup is ready to be served.

52. Ochazuke

Cooking Time: 5 minutes

Serving Size: 1

Ingredients:

- Dashi, one tbsp.
- Soy sauce, one tsp.
- Japanese green tea leaves, one
- Water, one cup
- Salt and pepper to taste
- Mirin, one tsp.

Instructions:

a) Combine all the ingredients in a small saucepan and bring it to a boil.
b) Pour the soup into a small teapot.
c) Put tea leaves in the pot.
d) Bring the water to the appropriate temperature for your tea and pour it into the pot.
e) Set aside for two minutes.
f) Your soup is ready to be served.

53. Ozoni

Cooking Time: 20 minutes

Serving Size: 4

Ingredients:

- Dashi, one cup
- Soy sauce, one tbsp.
- Sake, one tbsp.
- Chicken strips, one pound
- Water, two cups
- Salt and pepper to taste

Instructions:

a) Mix all the ingredients together and let it simmer.

b) Your soup is ready to be served.

54. Japanese Clear Onions Soup

Cooking Time: one hour

Serving Size: 5

Ingredients:

- Vegetable oil, two tbsp.
- Onion, one
- Carrot, one cup
- Garlic and ginger paste, one tbsp.
- Chicken broth, one cup

- Beef broth, one cup
- Salt and pepper as required

Instructions:

a) Place a large stock pot over medium-high heat.
b) Add the oil and place the onion, garlic, carrots, and ginger in the pot.
c) Sear the veggies on all sides to caramelize, making sure not to burn the garlic.
d) Pour in the chicken broth, beef broth, and water.
e) Bring to a boil.
f) Lower the heat to a low boil and simmer for at least one hour.
g) Use a skimmer to remove the vegetables from the broth.
h) Taste, then adjust salt as needed.
i) Your dish is ready to be served.

55. Wonton Dumplings Soup

Serving: 6

Ingredients:

- Wonton wrappers, twenty-four
- Finely chopped scallion, one tsp.
- Finely chopped ginger, one tsp.
- Soy sauce, one tbsp.
- Brown sugar, one tsp.
- Chicken breast, shredded, two
- Fresh spinach, one cup
- Shrimp, one pound

- Water chestnuts, eight ounces
- Mushroom, sliced, one cup
- Rice wine, one tbsp.
- Ground pork, eight ounces

Instructions:

a) Bring chicken stock to a rolling boil, and then add all the ingredients.
b) Cook until chicken and shrimps are cooked through, for about 10 minutes.
c) In a bowl, mix the pork, ground shrimp, brown sugar, rice wine or sherry, soy sauce, scallions and chopped ginger.
d) Blend well and set aside for 25-30 minutes for flavors to blend.
e) Add one tsp. of the filling in the center of each wonton wrapper.
f) Wet the edges of each wonton with a little water and press them together with your fingers to seal.
g) To cook, add wontons to the boiling chicken stock and cook for 4-5 minutes.

56. Kimchi and Tofu Soup

Serving Size: 2

Ingredients:

- Vegetable oil, one tbsp.
- Scallions, six
- Kimchi, half cup
- Chicken broth, one cup
- Soy sauce, three tbsp.
- Salt and pepper, as per taste
- Garlic and ginger paste, one tbsp.
- Tofu, one block
- Daikon, one

Instructions:

a) Heat oil in a large saucepan over high.

b) Cook white and pale-green parts of scallions, garlic, and ginger, stirring often, until softened and fragrant, about three minutes.

c) Add broth, then whisk in the soy sauce.

d) Add daikon and gently simmer until daikon is tender, fifteen minutes.

e) Add kimchi and tofu.

f) Simmer until tofu is heated through.

g) Carefully divide among bowls.

h) Your soup is ready to be served.

57. Shio Koji Mushroom Soup

Cooking Time: 20 minutes

Serving Size: 2

Ingredients:

- Soup stock, two cups
- Different mushrooms, two cups
- Salt and pepper to taste
- Shio koji, two tbsp.

Instructions:

a) Slice the mushrooms into thin slices or pieces and boil in plenty of water for about two mins.

b) Drain and add the shio koji seasoning to the hot mushrooms.

c) Wait about fifteen minutes for the flavours to develop.

d) In another saucepan, bring soup stock to the boil.

e) Add the mushrooms and salt and allow everything to heat through.

f) Spoon into bowls and serve with some nice crusty bread.

58. Yudofu

Cooking Time: 15 minutes

Serving Size: 2

Ingredients:

- Tofu, one block
- Mitsuba, as required
- Sake, one tbsp.
- Mirin, one tsp.
- Vegetable stock, three cups
- Water, one cup

Instructions:

a) Mix all the ingredients well and let it simmer for fifteen minutes.
b) Your soup is ready to be served.

59. Ojiya Rice Soup

Cooking Time: 20 minutes

Serving Size: 2

Ingredients:

- Japanese rice, one cup
- Vegetable stock, two cups
- Mixed vegetable, one cup
- Soy sauce, one tsp.
- Mirin, half tsp.
- Salt and pepper, to taste
- Water, two cups

Instructions:

a) Mix all the ingredients well and let it simmer for fifteen minutes.
b) Your soup is ready to be served.

60. Oshiruko Sweet Red Bean Soup

Cooking Time: 20 minutes

Serving Size: 3

Ingredients:

- Azuki sweet red beans, one cup
- Mochi rice cakes, four
- Vegetable stock, four cups

Instructions:

a) Start by adding the azuki and one cup for water to a large pan and bring it to the boil. You can adjust the amount of water depending if you prefer a thick or thin soup.

b) You can cook the mochi in a variety of ways, but grilling them gives great results so place the mochi under a hot grill for five to ten minutes.

c) Once the mochi begin expanding in the grill, they are ready and can be put into serving bowls.

d) After the azuki and water mix is boiled, take it off the heat and pour over the mochi in the serving bowls and enjoy.

61. Bean Paste Soup

Cooking Time: 15 minutes

Serving Size: 2

Ingredients:

- Bean paste, five tbsp.
- Vegetable soup, two cups
- Soy sauce, one tsp.
- Mirin, one tsp.
- Salt and pepper to taste

Instructions:

a) Mix all the ingredients well and let it simmer for fifteen minutes.

b) Your soup is ready to be served.

SNACKS

62. Japanese spicy white sauce

Ingredients

- 2 ¼ cup Japanese mayonnaise
- 1 ¼ tsp. garlic powder
- 1 cup. Ketchup
- 1tbsp. paprika
- 3 ¼ tbsp. sugar
- 2tsp. onion powder
- 1 ¼ tsp. cayenne pepper

- 1tsp. sea salt
- 1 ½ tsp. sriracha sauce
- 1 cup. water

Instructions

a) In a clean large bowl, pour in all the ingredients
b) Stir and beat well to mix till it is lump-free
c) Stand it in the refrigerator till you are ready to use it
d) Serve it with rice, pasta, or vegetable salad dressing

63. Japanese salmon and cucumber bites

Ingredients

a) 1 cucumber. Boldly sliced
b) ½ pound salmon fillet
c) 1 ¼ tsp. soy sauce
d) 2tbsp. scallions. Finely minced
e) 1tsp. mirin
f) 1 Ichimi togarashi (Japanese chili pepper)
g) 1tsp. sesame oil
h) ½ tsp. black sesame seeds

Instructions

i) In a small mixing bowl, combine the salmon, soy sauce, scallions, sesame oil, and mirin.

j) Place cucumber slices on a platter, spoon a scoop of the salmon on it, and drizzle remaining scallion and sesame seeds

64. Japanese keto-okra bowl

Ingredients

- 2 okra fingers
- 2tbsp. soy sauce
- 2tbsp. bonito flakes
- 2tbsp. swerve/monk fruit
- 2tbsp. water
- 2tbsp. sake
- 2tsp. sesame seeds, toasted
- 2tbsp. bonito flakes

Instructions

a) Boil 2 cups of water in a stovetop
b) In another cooker pot, stir in the soy sauce, bonito flakes, 2tsp. water, sake, swerve, and sauté for 1 minute
c) Return to the now boiling water and toss in the okra, cook for 3 minutes or till soft
d) Drain and chop into bold slices
e) Place the sliced okra in a bowl and pour the sauce over it
f) Garnish with sesame seeds and bonito flakes

65. Crunchy chicken with sauce

Ingredients

- 1lb boneless chicken thigh or breast. Cut into cubes or strips
- 3 ½ tsp. soy sauce
- 2tsp. freshly squeezed ginger juice (pound the ginger, add 1 tbsp. water and extract the juice)
- 3 tbsp. Japanese mirin
- ½ cup. Canola oil for frying
- 8tbsp. Japanese cooking sake
- 3tbsp. sesame seeds
- ¼ cup. Cornstarch

Instructions

a) In a large bowl, place chicken and season with the ginger juice, Japanese sake, soy sauce, and mirin. Marinade for 25 minutes

b) Drizzle the cornstarch over the chicken, making sure they are well-cover with the flour. Dust excess flour away and lay in a platter

c) Heat the oil in a skillet and deep-dry the chicken

d) Whisk together 3tsp. white miso paste, 3tbsp. mayonnaise, 3tsp. Japanese rice vinegar, or apple cider vinegar, a pinch of salt, and 2 tsp. honey

e) Bring out the chicken when cooked through and brown

f) Serve with the mayo dip or your preferred sauce

66. Japanese potstickers

Ingredients

- 1 ounce wonton wrappers
- 1 ½ cup chopped cabbage
- ½ cup. Asian scallions, chopped
- ¼ cup. Carrots. Chopped
- 1pound ground pork
- sesame oil
- 1garlic clove
- 1 garlic, finely chopped
- 1tbsp. soy sauce
- 1 ginger, grated

Instructions

a) Combine the pork, carrot, cabbage, sesame oil, garlic, soy sauce, and ginger till well incorporated.
b) Spread the wonton wrappers on a floured platform
c) Scoop a spoonful of filling onto the center of each wrapper
d) Moisten the wrappers with water and fold each into a wrap
e) Tweak the edges to make a pattern
f) Place dumplings in heated oil and fry till golden or cook in a steamer pot

67. Japanese teriyaki meatballs

Ingredients

- 1 (30ounce) pkt. frozen meatballs
- 1 (14ounce) teriyaki sauce or you make yours
- Cooked rice
- 1 cup pineapple bits

Instructions

a) Over medium heat, toss thawed meatballs, teriyaki sauce into a large skillet

b) Add the pineapple cubes and stir to mix. Turn off the heat

c) Scoop a sizeable portion of rice into a place and pour the ready meatballs over it

68. Japanese Summer Sandwiches

Cooking Time: 5 minutes

Serving: 2

Ingredients:

- Bread slices, six
- Strawberry, one cup
- Whipped cream, one cup

Instructions:

a) First you should prepare your bread.

b) Either whip half cup of whipping cream in a bowl until stiff and spread evenly on the bread.

c) Next, wash, cut off the stems and chop each strawberry in half down the middle.

d) Your sandwich is ready to be served.

69. Fresh Spring Rolls with Sauce

Cooking Time: 20 minutes

Serving: 4

Ingredients:

- Prawns, half pound
- Green beans, one cup
- Mint or coriander leaves, as required
- Rice paper wrapper, twelve
- Spring onion, half cup
- Mayonnaise, two tbsp.
- Bean chili paste, one tsp.
- Miso paste, one tsp.

Instructions:

a) Fill a small saucepan with some water and add a little salt.

b) Add the prawns and boil until they are bright pink for about five mins.

c) In a separate saucepan, boil the green beans for five mins.

d) Lay the rice paper on clean cloth.

e) Arrange the mint or coriander leaves on the bottom of the rice paper and add the prawn halves in the middle.

f) Top with the green beans and one whole chives or spring onion.

g) Sprinkle a little salt on top to taste.

h) Fold the sides in and tightly roll to ensure all ingredients are inside.

i) Make the dipping sauce by mixing all the ingredients together.

j) Serve spring rolls with the dipping sauce as a snack or side.

70. Karaage Japanese Fried Chicken

Cooking Time: 30 minutes

Serving: 6

Ingredients:

- Soy sauce, three tbsp.
- Boneless Chicken thighs, one pound
- Sake, one tbsp.
- Gaelic and ginger paste, one tsp.
- Katakuriko potato starch, a quarter cup
- Japanese mayonnaise, as required
- Cooking oil, as required

Instructions:

a) Cut chicken into bite-size pieces.

b) Add the ginger, garlic, soy sauce and cooking sake to a bowl and mix until combined.

c) Add the chicken, coat well, and allow marinating for twenty minutes.

d) Drain any excess liquid from the chicken and add your katakuriko potato starch. Mix until the pieces are fully coated.

e) Heat some cooking oil in a pan to around 180 degrees and test the temperature by dropping in some flour.

f) Fry a few pieces at a time for a few minutes until they are deep golden-brown colour, then remove and allow to drain on a wire rack or kitchen roll.

g) Serve hot or cold with some lemon wedges and a squeeze of Japanese mayonnaise.

71. Tazukuri Candied Sardines

Cooking Time: 15 minutes

Serving: 4

Ingredients:

- Toasted sesame seeds, one tbsp.
- Honey, one tbsp.
- Soy sauce, one tbsp.
- Sugar, one tbsp.
- Honey, one tbsp.
- Flavored oi, one tbsp.
- Sake, one tsp.
- Baby sardines, one cup

Instructions:

a) Gather all the ingredients. You will also need a baking sheet lined with parchment paper.

b) Put dried baby sardines in a frying pan, and toast them on medium-low heat for a few minutes or until crispy.

c) Add the sesame seeds in the frying pan and toast for two minutes.

d) Make sure to shake the pan constantly so the sesame seeds do not burn.

e) In the same frying pan, add sake, soy sauce, and sugar. Add honey and oil.

f) Bring to a simmer on medium-low heat and reduce the sauce until the sauce gets thicken and you can draw a line on the surface of the pan with a silicone spatula.

g) Add the sardines back to the pan and coat with the sauce.

72. Yakitori Grilled Skewers

Cooking Time: 10 minutes

Serving: 12

Ingredients:

- Teriyaki sauce, half cup
- Green shallots, two
- Chicken thigh, two pounds

Instructions:

a) Heat teriyaki sauce in a small saucepan medium-high heat. Bring to simmer and reduce to thicken the sauce.

b) Cut the white end part of the shallots into long pieces.

c) Prepare the skewers.

d) Preheat the BBQ grill and coat with olive oil.

e) Place the yakitori chicken skewers on the grill side to cook the chicken till browned.

f) Turn the skewers over and cook till other side browned or chicken meat change whitish colour.

g) Brush the Teriyaki sauce over the chicken skewers. When one side is coated, turn the skewers over and Brush Yakitori sauce over the side.

h) Repeat the above process one more time then turn the heat off.

i) Serve the yakitori skewers on rice or serve with green salad.

73. Sweet Ginger Meatballs

Serving: 4

Ingredients:

- Ginger and garlic paste, one tbsp.
- Eggs, one
- Ground turkey, one pound
- Sesame oil, half tsp.
- Soy sauce, four tbsp.
- Bread crumbs, half cup
- Hoisin, two tbsp.
- Diced scallions, as required
- Sesame seeds, as required

Instructions:

a) Pre-heat oven to 400 degrees and lightly grease a large baking sheet.
b) In a large bowl, add turkey, garlic, ginger, and mix well.
c) Then add egg, panko, sesame oil, and soy sauce, and mix well.
d) Roll out the meatballs and place on baking sheet.
e) Bake for ten mins and then rotate pan and bake for another ten minutes.
f) Transfer meatballs to a large sauté pan that will fit them all.
g) In a small bowl mix the remaining soy sauce and hoisin.
h) Coat and turn meatballs in sauce as it bubbles and thickens and let cook for a couple of minutes.
i) Remove meatballs, add to a bowl and pour remaining sauce on meatballs.

74. Satsuma Age Fried Fish Cake

Serving: 4

Ingredients:

- Sugar, two tbsp.
- Eggs, one
- Fish fillet, one pound
- Salt, as required
- Ginger juice, half tsp.
- Water, two tbsp.
- Mix vegetables, two cups
- Soy Sauce, one tbsp.

Instructions:

a) Cut fish fillet into small pieces so that it is easier to make paste in a food processor.

b) Add fish pieces, sake, ginger juice, salt and sugar to a food processor and whizz until the mixture becomes paste.

c) Add egg to the fish paste and blend well.

d) Add all the vegetable mixture in a large bowl and mix well ensuring that vegetable pieces are evenly coated with corn flour.

e) Add the fish paste to the bowl and mix well.

f) Heat oil in a deep-frying pan or a skillet to 170 degrees.

g) Take the fish cake mixture and make a ball.

h) Fry until bottom side of the fish cake is golden brown.

i) Remove the fish cake and drain oil on a rack or kitchen paper.

75. Nori Seaweed Popcorn

Cooking Time: 30 minutes

Serving: 6

Ingredients:

- Black sesame seeds, one tbsp.
- Brown sugar, one tbsp.
- Salt, half tsp.
- Coconut oil, half tsp.
- Popcorn kernel, half cup
- Butter, two tbsp.
- Nori seaweed flakes, one tbsp.

Instructions:

a) In a pestle and mortar, grind the nori seaweed flakes, sesame seeds, sugar and salt to a fine powder.

b) Melt the coconut oil in a large, heavy-bottomed saucepan.

c) Add popcorn kernels, cover with a lid and cook over a medium heat until they pop.

d) Immediately add the rest of the corn after the corn is popped, replace the lid and cook, shaking the pan occasionally until all the kernels are popped.

e) Transfer the popped corn to a large bowl and pour over the melted butter, if using.

f) Sprinkle over your sweet and salty nori mixture and use your hands to mix well until every piece is coated.

g) Top with the remaining sesame seeds.

DESSERTS

76. Japanese lemony shochu

Ingredients

- 20ml fresh lemon juice
- 20ml shochu
- 40ml soda water
- Lime and lemon wedges to garnish

Instructions

a) In a clean cocktail shaker, pour in all content and shake well to mix

b) Add some ice cubes into the ready glasses and pour the drink into each

c) Serve with lemon and lime wedges

77. Mochi sweets

Ingredients

- 1 ½ cup. Pre-made Anko
- 11/2 cup. water
- 1 cup. Katakuriko (corn starch)
- ½ cup. sugar
- 1 ¼ cup. shiratama-ko (rice flour)

Instructions

a) Heat ½ cup. Water. Add ½ cup. Sugar, bring to boil

b) Toss in ½ of the Anko powder. Stir well to mix

c) Add more water if it feels dry, stirring till it forms solid. Let aside to cool

d) When cooled, scoop content and mold into 10 or more small balls

e) Mix the remaining sugar and water in a small bowl, set aside

f) Pour the rice flour into a bowl. Carefully pour the sugar mix into the flour, stirring to form a dough

g) Place it in the microwave and heat up for 3 minutes

h) Spray some katakuriko on the surface, remove the dough, and place it on the floured platform.

i) Knead it gently, cut into balls and flatten each ball.

j) Place an Anko ball in each flat dough, roll it to form a ball

78. Japanese fruit skewers

Ingredients

- 2cup. Strawberry. DE hulled and tips removed
- 12 green olives
- 2 cup. Pineapple cubes or 1 can of pineapple
- 2cup. Sliced kiwis
- 2 cup. Blackberries
- 2 cup. Blueberries
- 9 skewers or toothpicks

Instructions

a) Drain excess fluid from the fruits and fix them alternatively onto the skewers
b) Arrange the stuffed skewers in a tray and sit in the refrigerator for 1 hour
c) Remove and serve when ready

79. Agar fruity salsa

Ingredients

- 1 stick. Kanten agar (fruit jelly)
- 1 small can. mandarin segments
- 40g shiratama-ko (rice flour)
- 3tbsp. pre-made red beans
- 10kg. sugar
- 1 cup. Mixed fruits of kiwis, strawberries, etc.

Instructions

a) Place the Kanten agar in cold water, allow soaking till it gets soft

b) Boil 250ml of water, drain the tender Kanten from water, and add to the boiling water. Add sugar to it and boil till Kanten is well dissolved. Pour into a bowl, allow to cool and freeze it in the freezer to set

c) Pour the shiratama-ko into a bowl, add some water and stir to form a dough. Roll it and cut into balls

d) Boil another large pot of water, add the shiratama-ko balls when the water boils and cook till the balls float above the boiling water.

e) Place the cut fruits in a bowl, add the ready shiratama-ko balls, scoop a portion of the red beans, mandarin, cut the set Kanten into cubes and add to the bowl.

f) Drizzle the mandarin syrup or soy sauce if available and serve

80. Fruity Japanese cup

Ingredients

- 1 can. sweeten condensed milk
- 1 can. Fruit (800g) cocktail. drained
- 1 bottle (12oz) kaong. Perfectly drained and rinsed
- 1 cup. Coconut meat. Finely cut to strips
- 1 bottle(10oz) coconut gel
- 1 (220ml) pack all-purpose cream
- 1 cup. Cheese. cut into cubes

Instructions

a) In a small bowl, mix the condensed milk with cream

b) Pour other Ingredients into the ready milk mixture. Toss well to mix

c) Cover bowl and chill for 3 hours

d) Remove from freezing and serve!

81. Japanese jiggly rice balls

Ingredients

- 70g Japanese rice. Cooked to tender
- 6tbsp. soy sauce
- 1lb cooked tuna

Instructions

a) Preheat grill
b) Scoop the cooked and cooled rice into your palm or use an onigiri mold to form a ball of rice.

c) Make an opening in the ball and add the filling, tuna, and close it back. (wrap as many balls as you can)

d) Grease the baking pan with cooking spray and place the balls into it

e) Grill it in a pre-heated oven for 12 minutes, turning occasionally till it is fairly tanned.

f) Remove from heat and paint with the soy sauce

g) Return to heat and serve!

82. Kinako Dango

Cooking Time: 5 minutes

Serving: 4

Ingredients:

- Kinako, half cup
- Granulated sugar, two tbsp.
- Cold water, half cup
- Dango powder, one cup
- Kosher salt, half tsp.

Instructions:

a) In a mixing bowl add Dango powder and water. Mix well until well combined.

b) Grab a little dough and shape into a ball.

c) Lay it on a plate and repeat until all the dough is used.

d) Set aside a bowl of cold water.

e) Add dango balls to boiling water and boil until they rise to the top.

f) Drain and add to cold water. Leave for a few minutes until they cool down and drain.

g) In another mixing bowl, add kinako, sugar and salt, and mix well.

h) Put a half of the kinako mixture in a serving bowl, add dango balls, and top with leftover kinako.

i) Your meal is ready to be served.

83. Japanese Style Pumpkin Pudding

Cooking Time: 25 minutes

Serving: 2

Ingredients:

- Pumpkin puree, one cup
- Sugar, three tbsp.
- Vanilla extract, one tsp.
- Eggs, two
- Gelatin powder, two tbsp.
- Maple syrup, as required

Instructions:

a) Dissolve the gelatin powder with the milk.

b) Meanwhile, put the pumpkin puree and sugar in a bowl, stir, and microwave on high for thirty seconds.

c) Stir in the milk and gelatin mix and add it to the pumpkin and sugar. Stir in the eggs and vanilla extract and combine well.

d) Get rid of the unblended bits left in the strainer.

e) Place a deep pan or pot over a burner and put the ramekins inside.

f) Turn the heat on and bring the water to a boil.

g) Turn the heat off and check the firmness of the puddings. The texture should be a little firm but still creamy like pudding.

h) Cool the puddings in the fridge until they are completely chilled.

84. Dorayaki

Cooking Time: 15 minutes

Serving: 6

Ingredients:

- Honey, two tbsp.
- Eggs, two
- Sugar, one cup
- Flour, one cup
- Baking powder, one tsp.
- Red bean paste, half cup

Instructions:

a) Gather all the ingredients.

b) In a large bowl, combine eggs, sugar, and honey and whisk well until the mixture becomes fluffy.

c) Sift flour and baking powder into the bowl and mix all together.

d) The batter should be slightly smoother now.

e) Heat a large non-stick frying pan over medium-low heat. It is best to take your time and heat slowly.

f) When you see the surface of the batter starting to bubble, flip over and cook the other side.

g) Put the red bean paste in the centre.

h) Wrap dorayaki with plastic wrap until ready to be served.

85. Fluffy Japanese Cheesecake

Ingredients:
- Vanilla ice cream
- Brownie mix, one box
- Hot fudge sauce

Instructions:
a) Preheat oven to 350 degrees.
b) Cut strips of foil to line jumbo muffin tin cups.
c) Layer strips in crisscross manner to use as lifting handles when brownies are done.
d) Spray foil in a pan with cooking spray.

e) Prepare brownie batter as described on the back of the box or according to your favorite recipe.

f) Divide batter evenly among muffin tin cups. Muffin cups will be about 3/4 full.

g) Place muffin tin on the rimmed baking sheet and bake in preheated oven for 40-50 minutes.

h) Remove from oven and cool in the pan for 5 minutes, then transfer to a cooling rack for ten additional minutes.

i) You may need to use a butter knife or icing spatula to loosen the sides of each brownie and then lift out of the muffin pan using the foil handles.

j) Serve warm brownie on a plate topped with a scoop of vanilla ice cream and hot fudge sauce.

86. Matcha Ice cream

Cooking Time: 5 minutes

Serving: 2

Ingredients:

- Matcha powder, three tbsp.
- Half and half, two cups
- Kosher salt, a pinch
- Sugar, half cup

Instructions:

a) In a medium saucepan, whisk together the half and half, sugar, and salt.

b) Start cooking the mixture over medium heat, and add green tea powder.

c) Remove from the heat and transfer the mixture to a bowl sitting in an ice bath. When the mixture is cool, cover with plastic wrap and chill in the refrigerator.

d) Your dish is ready to be served.

87. Taiyaki

Cooking Time: 15 minutes

Serving: 5

Ingredients:

- Cake flour, two cups
- Baking powder, one tsp.
- Baking soda, half tsp.
- Sugar, one cup
- Egg, two
- Milk, half cup

Instructions:

a) Sift the cake flour, baking powder and baking soda into a large bowl.

b) Add the sugar and whisk well to combine.

c) In a medium bowl, whisk the egg and then add the milk.

d) Combine the dry ingredients with wet ingredients and whisk well.

e) Pour the batter into a measuring cup or jug.

f) Heat the Taiyaki pan and grease the pan with vegetable oil using a brush.

g) Fill the Taiyaki pan mould about 60% full over medium-low heat.

h) Close the lid and immediately turn.

i) Then flip and cook. Open and check to see if Taiyaki is golden coloured.

88. Zenzai

Cooking Time: 15 minutes

Serving: 4

Ingredients:

- Mochi, one cup
- Red beans, one cup
- Sugar, three tbsp.

Instructions:

a) Place red beans, and five cups of water in a pot.

b) Bring to a boil and cook for five minutes, and then, strain the beans and discard the water they were cooked in.

c) Now, drain the beans, reserving the water they were cooked in.

d) Put drained beans into the pot, add sugar, and cook over medium heat for ten minutes, stirring constantly.

e) Then, pour in the water from cooking the beans, season with sugar, and stir over low heat.

f) Bake mochi over a grill or in a toaster oven until they expand and brown slightly.

g) Put mochi into a serving bowl and cover with a scoop of bean soup.

89. Okoshi

Cooking Time: 10 minutes

Serving: 3

Ingredients:

- Cooked rice, one cup
- Tempura oil, one tbsp.
- Sugar, one cup
- Puffed rice, one cup
- Peanuts, half cup

Instructions:

a) Spread the cooked rice on a baking sheet in a thin layer and place it on a flat sieve or a serving tray.

b) When the rice becomes translucent and crispy, it is ready for further preparation. First, break down any lumps using your fingers.

c) Line a mould for okoshi with baking paper.

d) Heat tempura oil to 180 degrees and deep fry the rice.

e) Mix sugar with water and cook over medium heat until the syrup starts simmering, then lower the heat and, if you wish, add peanuts.

f) Combine fried, puffed rice and sugar syrup quickly, and transfer to a container. Cover the top with a baking sheet, and press with a heavy and flat object.

g) Cut into small pieces and serve.

90. Dango

Cooking Time: 10 minutes

Serving: 6

Ingredients:

- Joshinko rice flour, one cup
- Shiratamako rice flour, one cup
- Sugar, half cup
- Hot water, as required

Instructions:

a) Mix together the joshinko non-glutinous rice flour, shiratamako glutinous rice flour and sugar.

b) Add the hot water little by little, mixing well.

c) Cover the bowl you mixed your dango mixture in and microwave for a few minutes. Dampen your hands again and roll the dough into evenly sized balls.

d) Your dish is ready to be served.

91. Kasutera

Serving: 24

Ingredients:

- Milk, one cup
- Honey, two tbsp.
- Flour, two cups
- Sugar, one cup

Instructions:

a) Set the oven to preheat to 170 degrees.

b) First, coat the bottom and the sides of a baking pan with butter or shortening, and then line it with baking paper, so that a portion of the paper is hanging over the sides of the pan.

c) Sprinkle the bottom of the pan with sugar.

d) Bring a pot of water to a boil, and then remove from the heat.

e) Whisk milk and honey together and double sift the flour.

f) Add the eggs and the sugar to the bowl.

g) Next, whisk in the milk and honey mixture, and then add flour tablespoon by tablespoon, whisking all the time until incorporated.

h) When the cake is cool enough to handle, put the cake into a plastic bag and seal. Refrigerate for a few hours.

i) Your dish is ready to be served.

RAMEN AND SUSHI RECIPES

92. Shoyu Ramen

Cooking Time: 30 minutes

Serving: 4

Ingredients:

- Chashu, one cup
- Nitamago, as required
- Shiitake, as required
- La-yu, as required
- Nori, half cup

- Ramen, four packs
- Dashi, half cup

Instructions:

a) In a pot of salted boiling water, cook ramen, stirring with tongs or chopsticks until cooked, about one minute.

b) In a small saucepan over medium heat, warm dashi and shiitake until barely simmering.

c) Cook for one minute and remove from heat.

d) Set shiitake aside.

e) Add dashi and noodles to serving bowl.

f) Top with chashu, nitamago, shiitake, green onion, a drizzle of la-yu, and nori, if desired.

93. Miso Ramen

Cooking Time: 10 minutes

Serving: 2

Ingredients:

- Miso paste, two tbsp.
- Mix vegetables, one cup
- Ramen, two packs
- Soy sauce, one tbsp.

Instructions:

a) Cook the ramen, and boil the vegetables.
b) Now mix all the remaining ingredients, and serve hot.

94. Simple Homemade Chicken Ramen

Cooking Time: 10 minutes

Serving: 2

Ingredients:

- Chicken, one cup
- Ramen noodles, two packs
- Oil, one tsp.
- Salt and pepper to taste

Instructions:

a) Cook the ramen, and chicken.

b) Now mix all the other ingredients, and serve hot.

95. Vegetarian Ramen

Cooking Time: 10 minutes

Serving: 2

Ingredients:

- Mix vegetables, one cup
- Ramen noodles, two packs
- Oil, one tsp.
- Salt and pepper to taste

Instructions:

a) Cook the ramen, and vegetables.
b) Now mix all the other ingredients, and serve hot.

96. Ramen Noodles

Cooking Time: 10 minutes

Serving: 2

Ingredients:

- Ramen noodles, two packs
- Miso paste, two tbsp.
- Soy Sauce, one tbsp.

Instructions:

a) Mix all the ingredients together, and cook well for ten minutes.

b) Your dish is ready to be served.

97. Pork Ramen

Cooking Time: 10 minutes

Serving: 2

Ingredients:

- Pork meat, one cup
- Ramen noodles, two packs
- Oil, one tsp.
- Salt and pepper to taste

Instructions:

a) Cook the ramen, and pork meat.
b) Now mix all the ingredients, and serve hot.

98. Instant Ramen

Cooking Time: 10 minutes

Serving: 2

Ingredients:

- Instant ramen noodles, two packs
- Instant spice mix, two tbsp.
- Water, three cups

Instructions:

a) Mix all the ingredients together and cook for ten minutes.
b) Your dish is ready to be served.

99. Tuna Sushi

Cooking Time: 5 minutes

Serving: 4

Ingredients:

- Sesame oil, half tsp.
- Green onions/scallions, two
- Toasted white sesame seeds, two tbsp.
- Spicy Mayo, two tbsp.
- Sushi rice (cooked and seasoned), one and a half cup
- Sashimi-grade tuna, four ounces
- Sriracha sauce, three tsp.

Instructions:

a) In a medium bowl, combine the tuna, Sriracha sauce, sesame oil, and some of the green onion.

b) Lay a sheet of nori, shiny side down, on the bamboo mat. Wet your fingers in water and spread $\frac{3}{4}$ cup of the rice evenly onto nori sheet.

c) Sprinkle the rice with sesame seeds.

d) Turn the sheet of nori over so that the rice side is facing down.

e) Place half of the tuna mixture at the bottom end of the nori sheet.

f) Grab the bottom edge of the bamboo mat while keeping the fillings in place with your fingers, roll into a tight cylinder form.

g) With a very sharp knife, cut the roll in half and then cut each half into three pieces.

h) Put a dollop of spicy mayo on top of each sushi.

100. Japanese Sushi Rolls

Serving: 4

Ingredients:

- Lemon, half
- Nori sheets, two
- Sushi rice, two cups
- Shrimp tempura, eight pieces
- Tobiko, two tbsp.
- Unagi (eel)
- Persian/Japanese cucumbers, one
- Avocados, one

Instructions:

a) Gently press the avocado slices with your fingers until the length of avocado is about the length of sushi roll.

b) Wrap the bamboo mat with plastic wrap, and place half of the nori sheet, shiny side down.

c) Turn it over and put the shrimp tempura, cucumber strips, and tobiko at the bottom end of the nori sheet.

d) From the bottom end, start rolling nori sheet over the filling until the bottom end reaches the nori sheet.

e) Place the bamboo mat over the roll and tightly squeeze the roll.

f) Using the side of the knife, place the avocado on top of the roll.

g) Place plastic wrap over the roll and then put the bamboo mat over.

h) Cut the roll into 8 pieces with the knife.

i) Put tobiko on each piece of sushi, and drizzle spicy mayo, and sprinkle black sesame seeds on top.

CONCLUSION

What a ride! Knowing awesome Japanese meals at once was worth the ride... and if you are planning on hosting an Asian-theme party, it is a good time to start practicing your Asian culinary skills and be proud of yourself. So, feel free to try your hands on them one by one and remember to tell us how it went.

Japanese Cuisine is known for its variety of dishes and its vast combination of rare spices that are usually grown only in Japan.

Happy Cooking Japanese Food!